CREATIVE ANTICS
FOR ROMANTICS

THE

LOVE

SCRAPBOOK

TOM DEVONALD

for a special one

Tom Devonald is UK-based
writer and graphic designer.

Known to his friends for his love of doodling and his
terrible memory. His main topics of interest are
psychology, design, philosophy and psychology.

Find out more at
tommydevonald.com

Published by Prion Books
20 Mortimer Street
London W1T 3JW

I HEART YOU

Give the book a new title to make it your own...

LIFE'S A JOURNAL, NOT A DISSERTATION

share your creations...

#THELOVESCRAPBOOK

PRION

MAKE LOVE

Somewhere in your house there is a pair of shoes that you've had for many years. (You may even be wearing them right now.)

You don't exactly remember buying them. They're not particularly cool. They kind of smell bad. You're not really running anywhere in them, but after years of wearing them they have slowly but surely morphed to the unique contours of your feet.

They have been with you through so many important occasions in your life and they've absorbed so much of your foot odour that they have evolved into a vital extension of you.

And DAMN they are comfy.

So comfy that you can't really put a value on them. You can't imagine life without them, and you'd be heartbroken if something happened to them.

Without getting too scientific, this is essentially how love works.

To achieve maximum awesomeness your relationship must be 'worn-in' in exactly the same way.

This book is designed to help with that process.

It will help you to creatively document your relationship, from when it's new, flashy, and box-fresh, turning heads everywhere you go, all the way up to couldn't-give-a-crap-what-other-people-think-worn-in-extreme-comfort-level...

Fill this book with your heartfelt sentiments and it becomes a piece of you, a reflection of your soul.

It's been specially designed to absorb your personality and the bits of your personality that have absorbed their personality; like an external hard-drive of romance or a kind of 'relationship horcrux'.

THIS BOOK CONTAINS
THE GREATEST LOVE STORY EVER TOLD... ...YOURS...
...ENJOY!

THIS BOOK BELONGS TO...

(write your 'BRANGELINA'
style name-mash here)

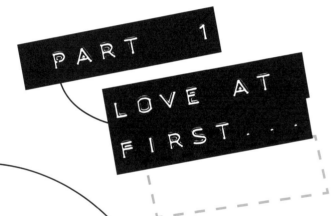

PART   1

LOVE AT

FIRST...

WARNING:

what people will think

'INSANE'

'CREEPY'

'ROMANTIC'

'CUTE'

'FUNNY''

How much of the book you complete

ALSO,

Whilst this book might become a hilarious catalogue of in-jokes for you and your co-dependent to laugh about, other people will not find it funny.

These 'outsiders' will find you gross and weird because they are not looking at the book through the oxytocin-tinted spectacles of a relationship; they are looking at it through the turd-tinted spectacles of loneliness.

This page is for marking the days
of your relationship

↓
𝍩

(like in prison)

A rose by any other name...

Please give your partner a <u>humiliatingly</u> luvvy-duvvy pet name (if you haven't already).

HELLO
my name is...

...Bear
...Boo
...Face
...Cakes
...Doll
...Doodle
...Boy
...Girl
...Cheeks
...Tits
...Pants
...Bunny
...Bug
...Pie
...Head
...Munch
...Drop
...Lips
...Love
...Buns
...Bunny
...Arse
...Bum
...Butt
...Legs
...Nose
...Pooh
...Monkey
...Biscuit
...Cookie
...Lamb
...Nugget
...ums
...kins
...bo
...Licious
...Beans

IF YOU'RE STRUGGLING TO THINK OF ONE, FEEL FREE TO USE A COMBINATION OF THESE TRIED AND TESTED NAMES

Cutie...
Angel...
Sugar...
Sweet...
Bunny...
Baby...
Babe...
Honey...
Petal...
Princess...
Queen...
Captain...
Prince...
King...
Stud...
Big...
Little...
Cuddle...
Dear...
Dimple...
Lover...
Goosey...
Gum...
Kitty...
Plumb...
Lolly...
Smelly...
Arse...
Cow...
Greedy...
Happy...
Sneezy...
Grumpy...
Munchkin...
Star...
Banana...

Now name and label any other parts of their __anatomy__ that you feel deserve a special mention

mark and date the
IMPORTANT MILESTONES
in your relationship

First
date

First
kiss

First
argument

Last ...

(celebrate these anniversaries)

when ▮▮▮▮▮▮ (Based
met ▮▮▮▮▮▮ on a true
story)

HOW WE MET...

HOW WE SHOULD TELL PEOPLE WE MET...

STAR-CROSSED LOVERS..?

check your star sign compatibility on a 'reputable' website.

(print out the results and stick them here)

it's.... Good news ☐

BAD NEWS ☐

Find a way of transferring your 'heart' line onto this page.

Then do the same with theirs over the top.

IS THERE A CORRELATION?

PART 2
THE HONEYMOON PERIOD

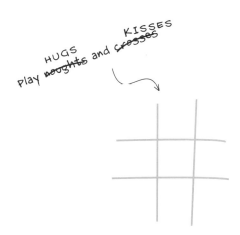

Play ~~Noughts~~ HUGS and ~~Crosses~~ KISSES

cover this page with pictures
of the two of you
(looking your best)

BLOW SOME KISSES ON TO THIS PAGE

then carefully tear it out
and fold it into a little
doggy bag, ensuring that
no kisses fall out.

Give it to your partner so that they
can unfold it later and rub the kisses
all over their face.

(you guys make me sick)

it's traditional to carve your initials into a tree.

This page USED TO BE a tree

(so it still counts if you carve your initials into it)

4EVA

Play 'join the dots'
on your partner's
freckles or moles.

Have you revealed any hidden
symbols that may indicate they are a
'chosen one' or a deity of some kind?

↑

Recreate any significant results

MAKE A COLLAGE GIG AND MOVIE

OUT OF YOUR OLD TICKETS HERE!

make little notes about memorable things that happened at the events on the tickets

which actors
would play
your parts in the ROM COM version
of your relationship?

....

and ....

Make a note of
any supporting
cast members....

. . . .

. . . .

. . . .

. . . .

. . . .

. . . .

. . . .

. . . .

. . . .

. . . .

Draw the movie poster here (what is it called?)

Jot down your
IN-JOKES
(summarise them in one word or phrase)

(Feel free to add any out – jokes that you use a lot around the sides here)

Do a LIFE DRAWING of them here.

This is a great opportunity to use your artistic licence...

(be generous)

make a record of any important scars or birthmarks they have.

(These notes will become important in the event of a homicidal clone situation.)

colour in your partner's most

TICKLISH AREAS

on these diagrams*

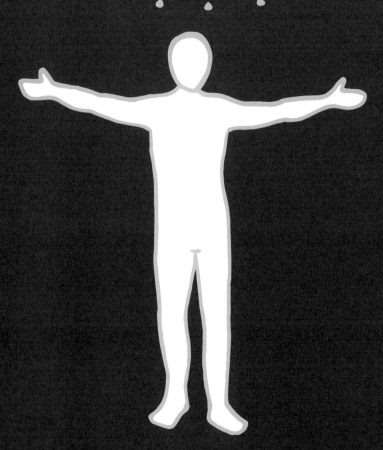

FRONT

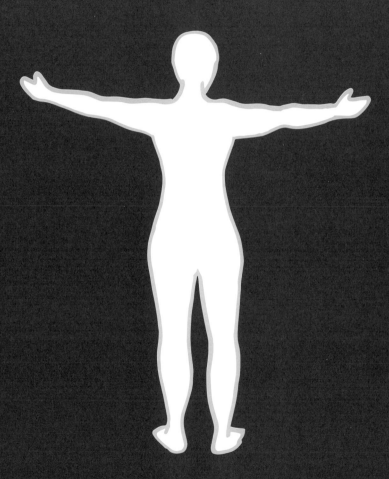

BACK

what would you call you and your partner's band? _____

what would your genre be called?

_____

DESIGN your band logo
on this T-shirt

create your debut album cover

FIRST GIG
set list

DRAW A
MAP
to their heart

what monsters are
lurking in the deep?

Please indicate the key reasons
you love them on this

HONEY-pie-chart

KEY REASONS KEY:

- ☐ _____
- ☐ _____
- ☐ _____

- ☐ _____
- ☐ _____
- ☐ _____

(List your reasons first, then assign a colour to each reason and colour in the pie chart)

LOVE
THEM

INDELIBLY

design some matching tattoos!... where should you get them?

what is
YOUR SONG?

....
customise
the lyrics

storyboard a new
music video starring
the two of you

Write them a note about something you did
together recently that was particularly awesome.

Now tear it out and hide it
SOMEWHERE THEY WON'T FIND IT
FOR MANY YEARS.

(This is GRADE A relationshipping.)

TRUE OR ~~FALSE~~ LOVE QUIZ

	true	false
	☐	☐
	☐	☐
	☐	☐

Complete these dictionary entries...

Romance (ro-manse) *noun:*

Love (lurrve) *noun:*

your partner's name goes here

( ) *noun:*

Fill these love hearts
sweets with messages
that only they will
understand

(If they truly love you
they will eat them upon
request to absorb the
raw power of your love)

Write
them some
fan mail

OFFICIAL
....
fan club
member #001

and wear this badge

what work of theirs are you particularly fond of?

cover this page in LIPSTICK KISSES
(if you're a guy then this gesture is even more meaningful)

Draw the
KEY TO YOUR HEART

make sure it looks badass.

Leave it in their possession.

Find a way of getting their delicious <u>smell</u> on to this page.

COMMUNICA-TION

PART 4

COMMUNINATOR C1000

Rip out this page and roll it
up to make a pea shooter
(the 'Communinator c1000')

Tear out these 'missiles', write messages on them and fire them at your boo with the 'communinator c1000'

make sock puppets of each other
and communicate through them
during arguments to add much
needed hilarity to your bickering.

"shall I compare thee to a summer's day?"

A summer's day is...

...but THOU art...

HOW MANY TIMES HAVE I TOLD YOU ?!

(Keep track of exactly how many
times you have told them below)

.... □ □ □ □ □ □ □ □ □ □ □

.... □ □ □ □ □ □ □ □ □ □ □

.... □ □ □ □ □ □ □ □ □ □ □

OFFICIAL-TOP-SECRET
CODE WORDS

.... = "I want to leave this crap party"

.... = "This guy is a douche"

.... = "This girl is an idiot"

.... = "I love you but I feel lame saying it right now"

.... = "Well this is an awkward situation we've found ourselves in"

.... = "I really wouldn't go into the bathroom right now"

.... = "You are an idiot and I hate you"

.... = "Darling, you are embarassing me"

.... = "Darling, you are embarassing yourself"

.... = "I am not the clone, shoot the other one"

.... =

.... =

.... =

.... =

These code words may just save your life.

If there's something you find it hard to talk to your partner about, attempt to communicate it through the medium of

INTERPRETIVE DANCE.

Report back with the results

_____
_____
_____
_____
_____
_____
_____
_____
_____
_____
_____

IN CASE OF EMERGENCY

RIP OUT

THIS PAGE.

(This is not a page.
It is a missile.)

(throw it at them when they
are refusing to listen.)

(then tape it back in here, you'll proabably
need it again pretty soon)

FREE

SELECTIVE

Hearing Aids

Use this page to make
ear plugs when they're
being annoying.

create your own unique

mating call

(and ritual)   *(Draw inspiration from the animal kingdom)*

(depict in the style of a cave painting)

KEEP THEM IN THE

Go through
your phone
and find their
funniest
texts to you.

PALM OF YOUR HAND

And your most
hilarious texts
to them.

write the (OPPOSITE) of how
you feel about them here:

be _specific_

attempt to draw your
feelings for them here...

for best results, take inspiration from
the abstract impressionists.

if that doesn't work, use glitter glue.

Write them a hint for self
improvement on this page.
Then rip it out and

DROP IT

(nonchalantly in their peripheral vision)

HINT HINT

CROSS WORDS

make a crossword puzzle on this page
where the answers are all insults you
would like to call your partner.

write the clues here ↓

DOWN

ACROSS

STEAL
something from
your partner.

make a ransom note out of this
page with letters cut from
magazines and newspapers.

what are your demands?

PART 5

HONESTY

Everyone knows <u>celebrities aren't real people.</u>

(That's why it's OK to cheat on your partner with one)

Fill in and cut out these cards

OFFICIAL CELEBRITY CRUSH CHEAT PASS

This pass entitles....

....

to cheat on...

....

with...

....

OFFICIAL CELEBRITY CRUSH CHEAT PASS

This pass entitles....

....

to cheat on...

....

with...

....

Keep your card on your person at all times so that when you meet said celebrity this stupid relationship thing doesn't ruin your chances of having their children.

WHO IS WINNING?

me ☐

them ☐

(for now)

create an exhaustive catalogue of their IMPERFECTIONS (if they have any)

loveable   ADORABLE

disgusting   enraging

Attempt to sell your partner on ebay

how much are they worth?

(show your workings-out)

 =$.........

write the advert here...

ARGUMENT
SCORECARD

Argument about...	WINNER!		
	player 1	player 2	DRAW

THE POWER
IN THE RELATIONSHIP

WHO HAS IT?

colour in the bars on different days depending on who is taking the lead. whoever has the most bars by the time the page is full officially rules the roost.

PLAYER 1

PLAYER 2

PILLOW TALK

create a colour coded diagram of who takes up the most space.

If you're no good at drawing, find two spoons (a big one and a little one)
and draw around them to show your relative locations.

I love you more than ....

but less than ....

THIS HEART REPRESENTS YOUR LOVE FOR THEM

Draw your love for other things
in hearts on this page (to
scale) until you have a scaled
infographic of the things
that you love.

THE MEAT

Things I would do for love

↓

_____

_____

_____

_____

_____

LOAF TEST

THAT

↓

_____

draw your relationship
as if you are a
SOLAR SYSTEM

who revolves around who? or are you binary?
what is at the centre?
what meteors are on the horizon?

BULLSH✱T THEM

1. Think of an outrageous lie to tell your partner about something that happened before you got together.

_____

_____

_____

2. (tell them)

3. Did they spot it?

NO

CONGRATULATIONS!
you are a criminal mastermind and you know them well enough to hoodwink them convincingly.

YES

CONGRATULATIONS!
you are with someone who knows you well enough to know that you are a weird liar but still stays with you anyway.

where is your relationship in relation to 'the rocks'?

(mark and date your location with an X)

(smooth sailing)

(rocky patch)

(the rocks)

what would the SITCOM about your relationship be called?

....

what are the catchphrases?

what is the theme tune?

create a fancy three-course
meal for your partner that
reflects their personality through
ingredients and presentation.
Glue pictures of the results here.

OFFICIAL CHORE DISTRIBUTION

LIVEN THINGS UP

chores are boring, why not cut out this page,
roll it up, tape it to your head and pretend to
be a unicorn instead.

(Impress your partner with
your magical new look).

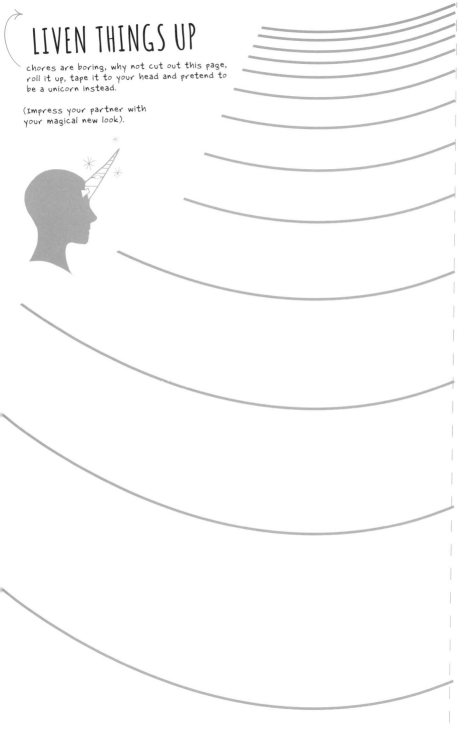

attempt to <u>SEDUCE</u> them

whilst

wearing

only

this

page

write a   m o t i v a t i o n a l
message to your partner here then rip
out this page and leave it somewhere
they will find it while they're at work.

↓

Write an instruction manual for how to operate your partner

(complete with illustrations and safety warnings)

PART 7

LETTING

YOURSELF

GO

COMPLETELY

cover this page with pictures
of the two of you
(at your worst)

Rate each other's burps out of 50...

LAYER 1

	Volume	Length	Power	Stealth	Hilarity	TOTAL

LAYER 2

	Volume	Length	Power	Stealth	Hilarity	TOTAL

The game resets when one person BURPS and FARTS
...AT THE SAME TIME

(burp-farting is the golden snitch of the burp rating game)

CONGRATULATIONS....
MAXIMUM COMFORT LEVEL ACHIEVED

create a

TROPHY

out of this page
and give it to
your partner

what is the award for?

....

Create an alternative to
Valentine's Day that is special
to the two of you and surprise
them with a card.

HAPPY .... DAY!

(Use this page if you want to be
a total cheapskate about it)

This voucher entitles:

....

to:

....

....

....

Single use only.

Terms and conditions apply.

Void if damaged.

Non-refundable.

use this voucher wisely

you are the ...Bill... to my ...Ted...

you are the .... to my ....

you are the .... to my ....

you are the .... to my ....

you are the .... to my ....

you are the .... to my ....

you are the .... to my ....

It's the little things

that count

write some of the
little things that you love
that they do on this page.
in your tiniest writing.

poetry is so 18th century

WRITE THEM SOME COMPLIMENTS
IN THE STYLE OF THEIR FAVOURITE
RAPPER

Attempt to 'entice' your partner whilst speaking in the following accents:

EASY

DIFFICULTY LEVEL

French ☐

Scottish ☐

Italian ☐

Spanish ☐

Irish ☐

Posh ☐

Australian ☐

Deep South ☐

Siri ☐

Cockney ☐

Scouse ☐

Dalek ☐

Birmingham ☐

IMPOSSIBLE

PART 9

KEEP THE SPARK

WIKI-PHELIA

1. Go to Wikipedia
2. Click on 'random article' (on the left)
3. Invent your own, ahem... 'intimate activity' based on the title of whatever article pops up.

Document your findings in the table below

Name of 'activity'	Instructions	Rating

PART 10

HAPPILY
EVER AFTER

find me attractive

Will you still ~~love~~ ~~me~~ when I'm 64?

Work out how ATTRACTED you will be to each other when you're old and grey with this finely-tuned measurement system.

> (1.) How attracted are you to THEM now?
>
> ..../10

+

> (2.) How attracted are you to their PARENTS now?
>
> ..../10

(3.) Divide the sum of these results by 2

=..../10

This is how attracted you will be to them when things go south

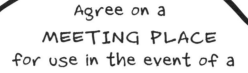

Design a
FAMILY
CREST
(include a motto)

WON'T SOMEBODY THINK OF THE CHILDREN?

Before you go any further in your relationship you should probably make sure you want the same things for your potential progeny.

HOW TO PLAY:

1/ Cut out this page and then cut it in half using the guides overleaf.

2/ Take one half each (boy or girl) and draw the first section of your ideal kid, (starting at the head).

3/ Fold over what you just did so that your partner doesn't see the child prematurely.

4/ Swap with your partner and allow them to draw the next section.

5/ When all sections are complete 'give birth' to your creations and discuss the results.

6/ Rethink your relationship (optional).

BOY ♂

Head and neck

Shoulders and torso

Crotch and top of legs

Legs and feet

GIRL ♀

Head and neck

Shoulders and torso

Crotch and top of legs

Legs and feet

BUT JUST IN CASE...

HOLLA
WE WANT PRENUP!

make a list of anything you have bought
together here and who gets to keep
what in the event of a break-up.

signed

....

....

Wondering what those weird pink lines are on the side of the pages?

Make a fold between the two highest marks, and again with the two lowest marks, on every page to turn your book into a 3D heart shape!

Visit my website for a video 'how to' guide.

wow! cool!

oh my!

If you have enjoyed this book then let's hope you never have to read...

(more of a 'love's crap book' than a 'love scrapbook')

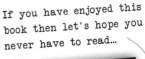

The Break-up Journal is the award-winning, interactive guide to surviving a split.

Get in touch with your dark side!
The Colouring Book for Goths is designed to help you cultivate 'a demeanour of aloof cynicism'.

Not to sound like, too desperate or whatever, but I was wondering, um, if you wouldn't mind adding me on twitter or instagram I guess?

It's just that I'd like to appear to have lots more friends than I do in real life because I'm deeply insecure. Also I design cool t-shirts and posters and put them on there or whatever so it's like totally win/win — for me.

instagram: tom.devonald

twitter: @pupilcreative

tommydevonald.com